FLY GUY PRESENTS:

BATS

Tedd Arnold

Scholastic Inc.

To Caroline Van Kirk Bissell,
the "Bat Lady" of the Chautauqua Bird,
Tree & Garden Club—T. A.

Photo credits:
Photos ©: cover: Yuzo Nakagawa/Minded Pictures; back cover: Dr. Merlin D. Tuttle/Science Source; 4–5: Brad J. Williams; 6: Mattias Klum/National Geographic Creative; 7 top left: Michael Durham/Minded Pictures; 7 top right: Dr. Merlin D. Tuttle/Science Source; 7 bottom left: Design Pics/Thinkstock; 7 bottom right: JohnPitcher/iStockphoto; 8 top left: Kptan123/Thinkstock; 8 top right: Pat Morris/Ardea; 8 bottom: Dr. Merlin D. Tuttle/Science Source; 9: Ivkuzmin/Dreamstime; 10 top left: Jason Edwards/National Geographic Creative; 10 top center: Mark Bowler/Science Source; 10 top right: B.G. Thomson/Science Source; 10 center: ER Degginger/Science Source; 10 bottom: FrankRamspott/iStockphoto; 11 top: OndrejVladyka/iStockphoto; 11 bottom: jasantiso/iStockphoto; 12: Super Prin/Shutterstock, Inc.; 13: Stephen Belcher/Minded Pictures; 14 top: Joe McDonald/Visuals Unlimited; 14 bottom left: Wil Meinderts, Buiten-beeld/Minded Pictures; 14 bottom right: the4js/iStockphoto; 15: Kim Taylor/Nature Picture Library/Corbis Images; 16 top: Mark Bowler/Science Source; 16 bottom: Dr. Merlin D. Tuttle/Science Source; 17 top: Tim Laman/National Geographic Creative; 17 bottom: Mealmeaw/Dreamstime; 18 left and right: Dr. Merlin D. Tuttle/Science Source; 19 top left: Michael Rolands/Shutterstock, Inc.; 19 top right: Dr. Merlin D. Tuttle/Science Source; 19 bottom: Nick Gordon/Ardea/Animals Animals; 20 top: Dave Roberts/Science Source; 20 bottom: C. Braun/Corbis Images; 21 left: Dr. Merlin D. Tuttle/Bat Conservation International/Science Source; 21 right: Michael Fogden/Animals Animals; 22 top left: Christian Ziegler/Getty Images; 22 top right: Christian Ziegler/Minded Pictures; 22 bottom: Ivkuzmin/Dreamstime; 23 top: Isselee/Dreamstime; 23 bottom: Stephen Dalton/Science Source; 24–25: Michael Durham/Minden Pictures/Corbis Images; 26: Ch'ien Lee/Minden Pictures/Corbis Images; 27 top: Stephen Dalton/Minded Pictures; 27 bottom: John Serrao/Science Source; 28 top and bottom: Dr. Merlin D. Tuttle/Bat Conservation International/Science Source; 29 top right: Roland Seitre/Minded Pictures; 29 top left: ER Degginger/Science Source; 29 bottom: Dr. Merlin D. Tuttle/Bat Conservation International/Science Source; 31 main and 31 inset: Christian Ziegler/Getty Images.

ISBN 978-0-545-77813-8

12 11 10 9 8 7 6 5 4 3   15 16 17 18 19/0

Printed in the U.S.A.   40
First printing, July 2015

A boy had a pet fly named Fly Guy.
Fly Guy could say the boy's name —

Buzz and Fly Guy went to the nocturnal (nahk-TUR-nuhl) house at the zoo.

Buzz looked at the map. They were inside a bat cave!

CREATURES OF
THE NIGHT MAP

= BAT
CAVE

= SWAMP =

"Bats are so cool," said Buzz. "But I don't know much about them."

Buzz and Fly Guy wanted to learn more.

Almost all bats are nocturnal. That means they are active at night and asleep during the day.

GREATER FLYING FOX BATS
SLEEPING IN TREES

Bats fly at night!

TOWNSEND'S BIG-EARED BAT

LESSER MOUSE-EARED BAT

BUZZ FLYZZ FUNNY!

RACCOON

BARN OWL

Other animals, such as raccoons and barn owls, are also mainly nocturnal.

Bats hang upside down to sleep. They hang in high places to be safe from hunting animals.

Some bats hang from trees or under bridges. Bats might even hang out in your attic!

FRUIT BAT IN A TREE

LONG-EARED BATS IN ATTIC

Other bats live in caves. They hang from the ceiling.

LESSER LONG-NOSED BATS

A group of bats is called a colony. Some colonies in caves have more than 20 million bats!

BAT COLONY IN CAVE

CAN YOU HANG LIKE A BAT?

EAZZY!

There are more than 1,200 different species (SPEE-sheez), or kinds, of bats!

tube-nosed bat

ghost bat

Jamaican fruit-eating bat

The most common bat in North America is the little brown bat.

little brown bat

Bats live on every continent— except for Antarctica.

the seven continents

They can be found as far north as the Arctic Circle, where temperatures can dip as low as negative 30 degrees Fahrenheit!

icy cave

They also live in very hot places, like Death Valley, California, where the temperature once reached 134 degrees Fahrenheit!

Death Valley

GREATER
FLYING FOX BAT
COAT OF FUR

Bats are mammals (MA-muhlz). Mammals
have fur and they are warm-blooded. That
means that the temperature of their bodies
does not change with the temperature of
where they are.

Bats are the only mammals in the world that can fly!

GREATER FLYING FOX BAT COLONY

I FLYZZ!

Yes, but you are not a mammal. You are an insect.

Flying is hard work! Bats use gravity (GRAH-vih-tee), or the force that pulls objects downward to Earth, to help them take off.

INDIAN FLYING FOX BAT

FRINGE-LIPPED BATS

BRAZILIAN FREE-TAIL BAT

First, bats hang upside down. Next, they drop from their perch and flap their wings until they are flying through the air.

● TOWNSEND'S BIG-EARED BAT IN STAGES OF FLIGHT ●

That is amazing!

YEZZ!!

Most bats are small and weigh less than two ounces. That is less than an orange!

scientist holding a ghost bat

Kitti's hog-nosed bat, also called the bumblebee bat, is the world's smallest bat. It is only about one inch long.

bumblebee bat being handled by a scientist

1 INCH

There are some large bats, too. The greater flying fox bat is the largest bat in the world. From tip to tip, its wings stretch to about five feet!

greater flying fox bat soaring through the sky

5-foot-long wingspan!

Different kinds of bats eat different things.

Many bats, such as the Egyptian slit-faced bat, eat insects. Some insect-eating bats also eat frogs, lizards, small birds, and even fish!

PALLID BAT

EGYPTIAN
SLIT-FACED BAT

EATZZ INSECTZZ?

I was hoping you would miss that fact.

Fruit bats munch on fruits and drink nectar from flowers.

PALLAS'S LONG-TONGUED BAT

EGYPTIAN FRUIT BAT

FRUIT BATS FEEDING

VAMPIRE BAT

Vampire bats eat only blood. They drink from other animals, such as cattle. These bats use heat sensors to help them find the animal they are hunting.

Bats have amazing bodies.

○ LONG-EARED BAT SKELETON ○

These small mammals have two wings, two legs, and a tail. They cannot run because their legs are too small. And their wings are not as strong as a bird's.

Bats have two thumbs—one at each wrist. These thumbs help them to climb, fight, and hunt.

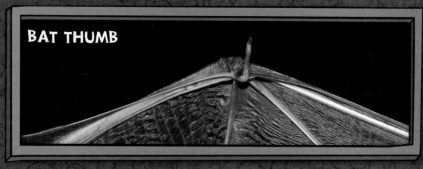

BAT THUMB

All bats have teeth. Fruit-eating bats have simpler teeth than bats that eat insects. Insect-eating bats have sharper teeth that help them crush insects. Vampire bats have razor-sharp teeth!

NICEFORO'S FOREST BAT

VAMPIRE BAT

Bats have super senses!

Some bats can see really well in the dark.

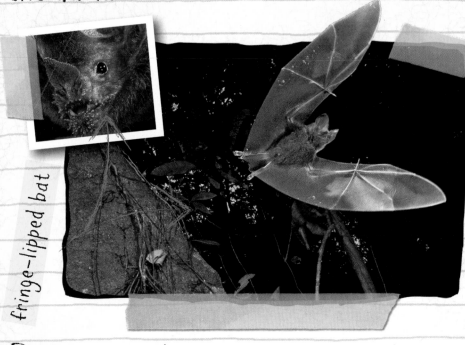

fringe-lipped bat

Bats' noses have extra-special smell sensors!

red flying fox bat

And bats have great hearing. They can hear an insect's beating wings!

WINGZZ MAKE NOIZE!

long-eared bat hunting a moth

grey long-eared bat

Many types of bats use a special sound to get around and to find food. This is called echolocation (eh-koh-loh-KAY-shun).

Bats send this sound out from their nose or mouth.

The sound travels to an object, bounces off it, and travels back to the bat's ears. This lets the bat know how far away the object is—so the bat can locate it.

Bat sounds are too high-pitched for people to hear.

Some bats make sounds louder than 110 decibels!

Not all bats hunt the same way.

Some bats, like the diadem roundleaf bat, wait for an insect to fly by. They then fly after the insect to catch it.

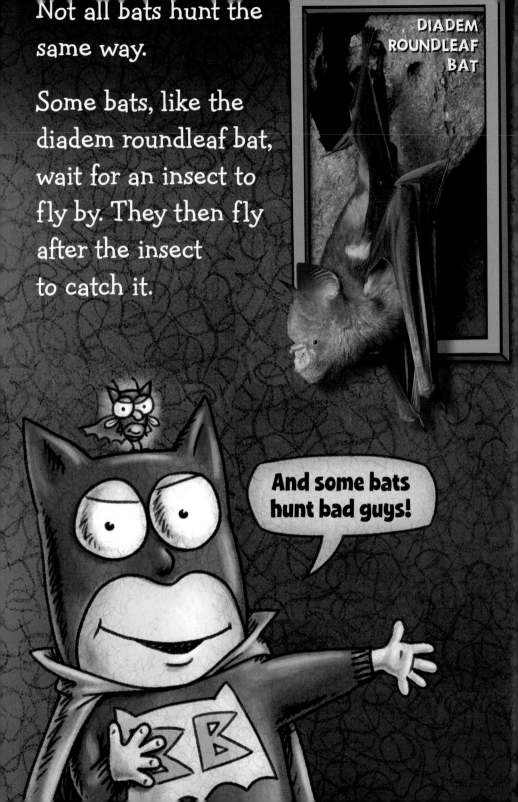

DIADEM ROUNDLEAF BAT

And some bats hunt bad guys!

Other bats hunt as a group. They help one another catch prey.

○ COLONY LEAVING CAVE ○

Many bats hibernate (HY-bur-nayt) in the winter when there is not much food. They go into a deep sleep. Then, when spring comes, the bats wake up to hunt again.

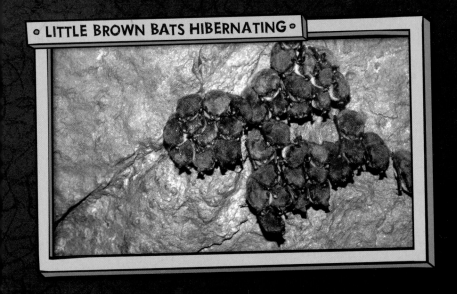

○ LITTLE BROWN BATS HIBERNATING ○

Most female bats give birth to only one baby each year. Baby bats are called pups.

PUPZZZ!

grey bat pup

All pups—even baby vampire bats—drink milk from their mothers.

Gambian bat mother and pup

Baby bats hang on to their mothers.

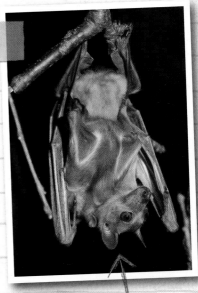

mother bats with pups

A mother bat recognizes her pup's scent and cry. Even with hundreds of pups in one colony, Mom can always find her baby.

fruit bat mother and pup

Chiropterologists (ki-KAHP-tur-AHL-uh-jists) are scientists who study bats. They try to learn more about bats.

CHIROPTEROLOGIST HOLDING A PALLID BAT CAPTURED IN A MIST NET

Chiropterologists look for new bat species.

DISK

In 2013, scientists discovered a new species of disk-wing bat. These bats have disks on their thumbs that help them to climb.

"Bats are amazing!" said Buzz. "From now on, I promise to never try to swat a bat, even if one gets in my house. I will get help to safely remove it. Bats are our friends."

Buzz and Fly Guy couldn't wait for their next adventure.